DIFFERENTIAL
DIAGNOSIS

DIFFERENTIAL DIAGNOSIS

POEMS

CAVAR

Curbstone Books / Northwestern University Press
Evanston, Illinois

Curbstone Books
Northwestern University Press
www.nupress.northwestern.edu

Printed in the United States of America

10 9 8 7 6 5 4 3 2 1

ISBN 979-8-89948-005-8 (paper)
ISBN 979-8-89948-006-5 (ebook)

Cataloging-in-Publication Data are available from the Library of Congress.

There are so many people, and they are so beautiful and hopeful. And they too are covered in holes. They each carry a bucket. And in each bucket is a hole. This is the song we're in.

—Sabrina Orah Mark, "There's a Hole in the Bucket," *Wild Milk*

watch
i will pull the rabbit from the hat, alive
            intact

—Evelyn Berry, "sloppy magician," *Grief Slut*

CONTENTS

PREFACE

Hi all. What a beneficent time. I hope you are doing well for yourself.

On this long long road why leave this make of the difference out to the cold the elements?

DIFFERENTIAL DIAGNOSIS (1)

There is a door at the center of myself.
That door belies the existence of many other doors.
This trend knows no sign of stopping.

(I dislike it. But it must be.)

I am really made of little vaults.
Vaults the color of my insides.

(My doors lead to the vaults.)

When things are not my fault I step through the door and close it in my
wake and in my wake I
close my eyes and say, well, none of it was my vault.

Luckily, my vault
is safe and full of goods. And only I can see it.
And all you see is text but I can see the outline of my vault.

My goods are little pieces.
They never exceed my skin. I stack them
every volume fewer than the last.

(My goods do not breathe oxygen.)

When I look I cannot find my goods.
My goods are gods whose holes can't fit a finger.

I am chronically holy.
This is not healthy under any circumstances.

I call my goods my precious gods because I cannot see them.
When I look I find my subtle vault
alone and faith the difference,

like I just believe electrons
fear arrest
by laws of physics.

OOOOOOO PROVIDER

Presider
Choke me only
In the beautiful way

AUTOMYTHOLOGY (1)

The tubes made pigeons of us. Nothing like a great hole
 out of subholes. In the land of the living are thought
the notion of holes sacred and discreet. Inside, holes merely
small tunnels of a Tunnel. No limit to what may pass / find
a way out.

Can you help me pass into a new mythology?

A SMALL SOMETHING (1)

If you get too close it will throat you.
It lives in the stomach and the choke
It colt-ankles skillfully
Crosses the dining table
Commits a murder.
That is. A house

DIFFERENTIAL DIAGNOSIS (2)

The name of this thing has no name.
The name of this thing is hard to pronounce.
Announcing this name is like saying I'm sorry.

Do you hear the world jumping on the backs
of other worlds. And find unjust. Do you sit silent
as the people like you are silenced? What is held

accountable. What is reckoning. What is the numerical value
of this thing who has no name. What is it called

When the monster does not come at nighttime.
What is it called when the monster enters
unannounced. To have no

Name is to have no announcement
no press briefing no substantive
counterdiscourse. I believe I have

No name but rather perhaps dent or
event   This thing remains nameless
a thing the size of an ocean, the ocean, the only

Ocean which is all notions, married as they are
by rivers of arbitrary
breaks and lots and damming. This thing

sends me into dark places
where the nameless live. When I open the box
that lies

Between my flesh and my bone I locate
a dark space. You cannot read in there.
You cannot give her a name. She is meant
To be a darkness and yet in this nameless darkness I am holding my
hand and rigging my terror.

SELF-PORTRAIT AS A SOUR JAR OF PICKLES BURIED DEEP BENEATH THE EARTH

No. There is no light in me.
That glow was just my chewed-
up swallowed-down came-out sort of
heat—

No. I am not about
to purchase of your
lightness.

No
not even
when my juices
look otherwise
like sun

No! I can NOT   both
see and butter
at once
such senseful & mercible beds!

I am sick
to fuck of being sensible!

I am sick
to fuck of light!

I am sick to suck of right
all when I asked
for aspect!

CONFESSIONAL (SCENE 1)

when I was small,
I wanted the world
inside of me. Now
that I am smaller,
I want to give
myself back

to speak myself
in its *langue* its
skinny *langue-
langage* my skin

went to the doctor
before I went
every route I could
Google without
whipping up the
sus on this
intern et of
things I can
turn sus up like
unwashed

greens my old
things my
deepmold
my gain a
savage sense of
pleasure love
the way it makes
me ache down
there love the
double entendre of
the way it feels
inside

DIFFERENTIAL DIAGNOSIS (3)

I have been sitting at your table for years now.
I am making an appointment with fate.
I can hardly stomach all the cashews you are feeding me!
I can hardly mind the milk when biscuits are still to be found.
I believe fat e is a thing that can be tempted.
I am not sure you understand me clearly.
I am not sure this strange little world contains a noose.
I do not think anyone I know smells fear.
I believe fear exists inside the odor I offer you.
I think my own capacity for living has somehow inhibited—
I tore my sugar box at the seams.
I tore the scenes up, and the curtains too.
I do not exist outside specific contexts.
I cannot read or write.
I can stop hurting myself if I try harder.
I pull harder on this mantle and
I burn the text alive.

ELEPHANTS THINK THEY ARE THE SIZE OF DOGS

Who can fault them, outwitting their great heft? And I am the size of Grammy's voice at the burnt crack beneath her knife. Her grandmother, Mème, would eat two toasts per day, no grease, between her prayers alone. Face against the floor. Grammy takes hers with coffee and a Camel. An earlier version of this piece contained incriminating information on   but I got rid of her. An earlier draft of this piece contained incriminating information on

1

2

3

4

Grammy   once described clothing as forgiving and I imagined a wardrobe built only by resentment. She spoke between smokes of her deathdream: a forest, a fuck, a rainstorm, alone. I can't breathe around you, granddaughter tells her fore. Now you are a feather bed. Now I am a rib. Who can fault me for outwitting my body.

---

1. having gone the distance as it were from the scene
2. of which dried up carbon, or perhaps the sound of scraping
3. hitherto unknown but as measure of license
4. and perhaps local to the knife or even the greed

WET MISTRESS (AUTOMYTHOLOGY 1.5)

buzz buzz! The aperture of this day is a father.
Hence his razorforce, hence the name of the blade.
Perhaps his greatest skill is cutting. Cutting and burying
you a gourd in this fallow this sparse
anemic earth.

Here is a world, desperate
for a calorie. Here is a language gone brutalforblood.
I am told when I hurt, let it,
but the blood stays blue with the shock

of the chill of my sallow
Skin begs the beetles to lay their eggs
down to lay their anysignoflives
Inside my cruel   inside my father

& I   both vie
for the same

daughter.

DIFFERENTIAL DIAGNOSIS (4)

to name

to have been good &
named

into clouded
waifish

distress

SOS

send okay
send me to that great sad
struggling world of things
yes yes[1] oh ah yes!
my body brim
w worries they wing w
mothpow er

leak w
beetles

fly like desire2
mouth

this crystalline pill
glows long beneath my
diaphragm

---

1. Hannah Emerson, *The Kissing of Kissing* (Milkweed Editions, 2022)

DIRECTOR'S CUT

The difference between fasting and starving is context. Context refers to the texture of that which is woven together. Years in the making. As a child I dreamed of weaving challah braid by braid to diamond-crusted egg-beaten beauty. This, from the first moment at my grandmother's house, when I learned how bread could big me in unexpected ways. I put on makeup in her bathroom and set out to eat, my context humming, warm, smelling of cheese and chips. We watched *Survivor*, saw irony to pieces. The longer they survived, the whittler they got. Men's stomachs sank beneath their hip bones. Women hunched above their coconuts, prey to break next-fast fish-flesh. In this context, survive means the getting some guts with a spear. And hyponatremia.

THE WAYS OF THE MONSTER

(after Jay Besemer)

Marched bloody brooding into
This blanched cruel universe

the Monster opens
bad eyes.

I hold Monster stillborn-close
Warn the angle

of its cries.

We are clipped pigeons
in the gutter.

I am holding like a bird.
Wandered and returned.

Monster we together
Ending nations. Eating

breakfast. Archive
the long arc of longing.

I have wandered and returned

in the

of a swallow.

We are in the gutter.
Someone narrows the aperture.

WHEN I TASTE BLOOD

my mouth don't see it
as a bad thing.

See, every night I affront the mirror
w/ sordid tales of glorified
flossing.

So ask me: Does all my narrow
make this teeth look fat?

/

I don't know

about you, but I was born in the wrong
episteme. My contrite gums
are cherry, jaw fusty.

&thus my slutty canines make lust
to the sound of tribbing
paradigms.

&thus I have cavities in my
cavities and also many
unofficial holes.

CONFESSIONAL (SCENE 2)

on the eve of my commission I read a vampire book and it was comforting, because when you think about it, being a vampire is just a big ole eating disorder. There were just then many unknowns in my life and even more diversions but they were good they made me everything but dead and in that way twice as killable

many theories exist as to what happens when vampires can't get blood. And if they get human food instead. Instead of looking them up, I invite you to think up a summer: you've forgotten how to leave. you've forgotten how to heat. you've even forgotten how to masturbate, or whether or not you're supposed to. you traverse the raw summer landscape, find a proud bird. the bird gets you shit-faced, except you're sober. the white sucks no blood but still comes from a body.

HALF-FORMED GIRL NARRATIVE

Take me backward into that
the dark world of myself.

Sidledare remove me from the light-beings
Sidlequick disapprehend the body

From their quick encurdled
Thumbs. Together a dreaming

a world without milk, bones in
venting chalices of seismic range.

Someplace where the babies
elsewhere got the lie

-down dead ditch dirt
wormfood wrinklestrain bodyminds

Tossed into their weathering yummy
language   angels eat

The title is after Eimear McBride, *A Girl Is a Half-Formed Thing* (Galley Beggar Press, 2013).

AUTOMYTHOLOGY (2)

Let's say I'm a monster. Say poetry made me this way. Let's say words are monsters trying to become sentences. Let's say it's pathological, I try to see my spine too much. Let's say I'm wondering if there's something waiting under there. Waiting I mean waiting to bust out. Let's say I am slumping for some good reason, that I have cut off my head and fallen in love with them and they have fallen back for me. Let's say it's enough. Let's say my contortions really check for wings.

DIFFERENTIAL DIAGNOSIS (5)

I'm sorry for subdividing.

Sorry for
Faster not stop.

In sorry my sorrys a plural.

Which my mechanism
At the grand scale. Yes

I'm worries I
        worries   my sorrys
Swear angst is wrung and wet.

Look: I wish I do not have to be this way.
That my moisten would normally.

Or perhaps that there's a hack
for that.

A slim trick for it.
goofy junk thing   I am

MISE-EN-SCÈNE

I. Interpellation

The man chased me from park to park. From each park he climbed a tree. From each tree he vindicated me. I, bare-chested, fearless, legged, panting, breaker of the rule of three, sped the sidewalk like a racetrack. He always seemed to abdicate the tree to me, event in front of me a large old pillar. He shouted in a language I hardly understood. I shouted hardly back. When he came to grasp me I was gone, gone because he didn't have a name for the thing he attempted hands on. The park opened to a walk of bicycles and speeding cars; I crossed them each until a haze of better people. He nowhere to be found.

II. Ideology

The barbershop vented me from the door. That is, it evented me. I am looking for a hare-share, I mean hair-shorn, I mean, I stumble to the man behind the hair-chair, bits scattered about the floor. He looks with big dark eyes at my little face. I am wearing the right shorts and the right wad of sock. I am even wearing sneakers. We are closed, and my eyes sweep the emptiness. May I make an appointment. Please consider the shop across the street, he claimed, pressing a molting business card into my hand. It continued to molt until it, too, was hair. I sow bare my head the exit window.

III. Apparatus

A thirty-years of hand against my nighttime scar. Is everything okay, breathed against my core. Yes, I check the door, I beg of silence. I beg against her finger. I bag above her head. Everything you find I have already found. I am. All is well.

PRINCESS NARRATIVE

When it strikes twelve I might well be a normal girl.

I think when it strikes twelve I will want to rip fewer flesh from myself.

The basal tremors of that putrid cause

my blood pressure.

DIFFERENTIAL DIAGNOSIS (6)

Okay, epistemology:
The story of the fuzz
On my lip. The backbreaking
Labor of being born, nay,
Of being known.
The manner of pimping
The body to the dictionary,
Or worse, the man
ual. The fucked
-up travesty lays
its egg in
definition. You want
to feel how it feels?
You want to hit
the embassy of my
Name? Cool, try this.
Open your fridge. Gloat
Yourself in cold. Invent a value
-system as consistent as
nonsensical. Event
milk. Event crisis. Event
horizon. State the beverage
as if it knows your secret
Name. As if Name's sat
Slack-heavy inside the
Great flat whiteness. You know
The milk risks reifying you
for good. Now,
What are you going to do?

DIFFERENTIAL DIAGNOSIS (7) (HAZE EDITION)

I say hello to the haze I say hello haze haze
asks can you
learn to love
me I say what
is love haze tells
love is when you
feel your heart is
flaying did you
mean flying I
mean flaying
out of your
body I believe I
am in love with
you I say the
haze agrees the
haze the haze is
flays my heart
in savage affect

DEATH PRACTICE

So many things feel
Closure's all
Liver beside
Outside my door
(Like strangling)
Two
(Of two)
Ringing on doorbells.
closures
(Opposites)
Close of all meaning—
The Liver is the organ of

like strangling:
chopped
the point.
doors are
persons,
but really, the opposite
blue shirts, knocking /
rapping
tight, chopping
as if draining
poison from
a door.

DIAGNOSTICIAN'S NOTE

Some are learned
in the ways of panting.

Some leather gestures
wail.

You are a student of your own body:
Pleasure the selected photograph.

Derive the side table.
She can't stand

In her obstinate
obstinancy.

—is bleeding
From the bedroom.

Ask me:
        What constitutes a victim
        -less crime?

Nothing is benign when laced
within your spinal warfare.

You are not immune

To conceptual frameworks. Not even
The ones that bring out

Your eyes.

SUBSTITUTION POEM

The stick figure is in crisis*!
The stick figure has become severe in her self*.
Help the figure regain
Her composure*.

I think you've seen her* in the pictures.
I don't blame you in your stark and honest
posture! My long*
makes a dire scene*

Particularly* at the site of the great calorie

(To speak the calorie*
Is to scene this savage fireset*), and to make
The * as tenured like a father

To substitutional* be
Upon plenary* of
Upon penalty of Death*

Appropriate Substitutions:

A. fugue
B. shape
C. hand
D. ______
E. salvage

CONFESSIONAL (SCENE 3)

I have a waifish problem. I used to be agnostic. I'm now Uncool With Food. Spent years hauled to the diner every Saturday afternoon for drink big strawberry milkshake with whip and maraschino and eat a two-egg spinach-feta omelette with a hash brown slab and butter rye toast just eat all down like it was there in my organs or my job put it all back inside as quick as I could. That's always how I ate perhaps hasty, like haste was a paste back then. Fast. Fast that slicked all that shit right no season.

DIFFERENTIAL DIAGNOSIS (8)

You spot my wrong a while
away. You may

Get even to name it, for good
Or ill. You see

In the ways of my coffee
Drunk as if somewhere

There is a hole and i am trying
To climb inside. Or the whole

Is like a thing preclaiming
Me claiming me prior

To the name of the claim.)

//

Get my name and fuck me
with it.

I delight with delicious
Literacy.

I am this savage pleasure. dirty
Mushroom in my mouth. Sarah she

Can't come unless you spit loudloud.

CHANGELING NARRATIVE

When I was young I held my pencil
in a balled fist.

This is not a metaphor.

I sport a chipped tooth
Between my thumb and index finger   it prepares

My capacious extraction.

I am not sure I believe in all the things wrong with me.
I know just that I am a cat person: accustomed
to cohabiting alone.

(If I am lucky this torment
ed catalog of sadness will

Carry on!)

This mountain I have considered.

I have considered subsisting this mountain.
I have considered submitting this mountain.

I have considered summiting this mountain
and

impressed each

star   I am am
igara fault.

My mind is a map of this perfect body.

I determine to method so beautiful and rapturous
break   my   hors[1]   bit
by sorry bit.

1. Jos Charles, *feeld* (Milkweed Editions, 2018)

PREY ANIMAL

I used to be a nest
I am a victim of the
pronouns babybirds
Eatingeating[1] at my stray

skinwoman builds her toolong
body up from the eczema earth
I rub myself
Into a pile for her food

Is a stunning rejoinder
I meet at the edge of my story
I mean at the edge of my gut
When there could be acid

Eating as whether form or
Function—

A strange beastfox stalks
The babies made of skin I spin
A trail of bad attitudes for eating
At the sticks I no longer gather

for when the babies are gone
they are gone when not
used

---

1. After Kim Hyesoon

I WRITE YOU FROM THE HOLLOW

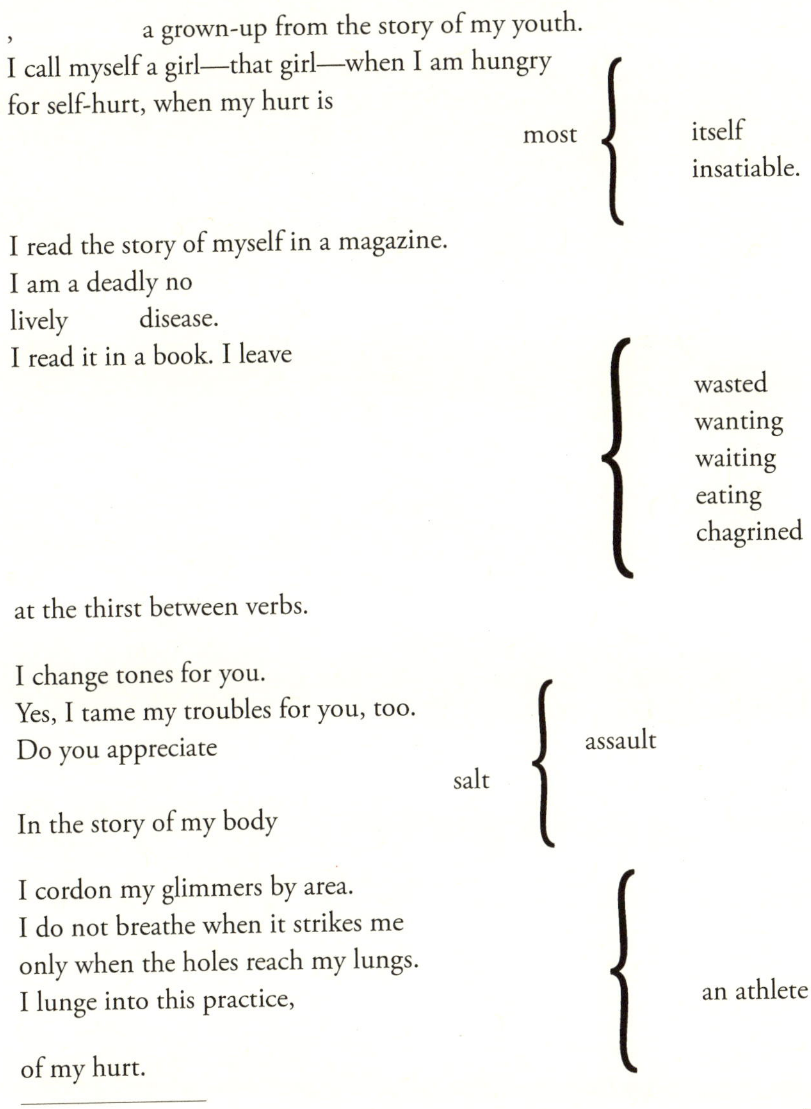

"The manifest discourse, therefore, is really no more than the repressive presence of what it does not say; and this 'not-said' is a hollow that undermines from within all that is said." Michel Foucault, *The Archaeology of Knowledge, and The Discourse on Language*, trans. A. M. Sheridan Smith.

HAVE YOU SEEN MY AUTISM?

It all started
when I was born.

Worse yet, it started
on the taxpayer dime

In the bathwater, in the atmosphere, even

in the baby
if a baby

can get tall enough for college.
It's true, I am autism

But only when you ask
nicely.

My autism is gentle, yet growing
carnivorous.

Like Medusa, my autism
is something you maybe

shouldn't see,

but if you do, you should
write a book about.

Someone told me

if a flower opens
wide enough

it just becomes a backward
flower.

Sanded teeth become new teeth,
renarrated to points.

With enough training, I'm sure

I can make a point
myself, I can

settle on a sex
for this my waspish swarm.

Be whatever gentle in

tends itself to mean,
though I've been nouns

that would kill you
instantly.

I am autism, if you're

willing. Autism,
if you're down—

Gentle, I'm a horny orchid
impervious

to pest control.

This autism's so long
it's forgotten

how to stop.

DIFFERENTIAL DIAGNOSIS (9) (INTERVIEW WITH A VAMPIRE)

I like to think I am a very good sport about [gestures]
all of this.
Such as being okay with the blood on my sweater when
you bit me
even though you promised me
you weren't a vampire. You were telling the truth, anyway,
but still couldn't help wanting a piece of this neck.

DIFFERENTIAL DIAGNOSIS (10) (TRANS ED)

You don't eat the food.

You have been papers a long time today.

You burnt a lucky fire in the gowngullet.

~~Text alive in flame emits a nasty shadow.~~

Just lie back and think about it.

Just lie back and think about other things.

Just lie to the sheer evidence of fire.

MY FIRST CRIME

I am have never been cage-free. Always compensating for something.
I once climbed a tree the borderline my childhouse and backyard
neighbors' / passed the horseshoe-ring and goldenrod and property-line.

> Passed the unwatched horseshoe-ring and goldenrod.
> Landlording rocks kept watch over the property-line.
> It is unwise to the edge of one's enclosure.

I am always compensating for something. Afraid I had no place to hide,
I climbed, unbearable pain in my ankles. Other Mother calling from her
window. *How can she bear the weight of her own gravity*

> I existed to an unbearable pain
> In my ankles. But that's not all.

I heard my neighbors' father was a policeman, so I spent my yard afraid I
had no place to hide.

> Every house was made of shouting-trees, and every house could talk!
> Every shouting-tree was a policeman coming home
> from work!

So I joined the trail of occupants who probably hadn't horseshoed since
1977. I began to blaspheme loudly as a form of self-soothing.

> I continued hearing strange voices inside
> voices metal round my neck
> Chafing even through my feathers.

> In a panic, I had swallowed Other Mother!

In a panic or maybe a/shame. Either way, Other Mother got stuck
mid-throat   and protruded, cop with his gun turned sights on me.
In my tree. I wave from my tree. I wave in the wind. I warp and weft,
winded.

Cage-free requires the preexistence of cages.
A border cages both ways, but only one that matters.

ENVY NARRATIVE

Whatever, a pasty fugue.
Heartburn. Fatigue.

I'm not so great, but I'm drilling
wherever I go.

The first dent's inside me. And out
on its own time.

My party figure, I mean
my pasty

fugue

Is not responsible for my feelings.

I have myself to blame. She can't
Be trusted.

(Envy enters on its stolen
bicycle.)

//

Here is a story with weight:

Once my legs swelled so big I was sure the fluid would burst

From my little red hairbearing holes.
I was round-ready to emit

dyingfluids like a crushed bug.

But didn't.

And so imagine my surprise upon the doctor.
My sedentary archive to blame. I mean,

My cemetery arrives on the hands of a bike
and scream of the break. Do you understand?

Every wheel is a hole that is possible. And resolves at times
with me inside.

IMPEDIMENT LITANY

(for Mel Baggs &after the month of **april**)

autistic in the mouth
autistic in the month of the cruel joke.

autistic in the stomach of my butterflies
autistic in the chapping

of the solar plexus.
autistic all along

the bias grain.

autistic in the width of my survival
-mode. yes yes even

autistic in the fucking
architecture.

autistic in this chicest kennel.

autistic in the veritable codex
of bad ideas.

DIFFERENTIAL DIAGNOSIS (11)

my name is the sick of my illness. i am good
and named in the thick of my illness. sick

in my illness. yes thick sick sickin my illness.

siccin my illness. i grasp this illness this im
perative like a cold cruise animal

EMAILS FROM THE MONSTER

//

don't hurt yourself if you are not going to die of it

//

you   nothing
but archive precariously pitched
perched apoplectic   thick   as the fur

[carries
[dirt]]

is a diet onerous enough 2fit your desire?

//

there could be a store big enough to archive you, but like why,

why   why bother

//

someone hope this message find you worst for
where

A SMALL SOMETHING (2)

alights
beside in bed. a small
Torch flickles the wanting.
a small something glews
w fleas & lines

a sweater
with delight sweats a body
full of feud a clinging
shapegrammar shift

a small something

does not look fine
repeat
Does not look fine
In that in that in

a small something

a mere mechanism
of subterfuge: step one
commit, step two
refuse

step three:
indicate
in the pick of litter,
a smallself

ALICE NARRATIVE

I fear I have been dropped into the wrong story.

I fear I have been led into the wrong story
at knifepoint.

It is easier to be un- than wrongly wired.
Still easier to swallow this life like a dog.

Sometimes

Being born wrong is a gift.
In such doggydog worlds we may

We'll die before we can be killed.

Several downtrodden women file me into sharktooth necklaces.

[NAME*] CONFESSES A PASSING FANCY

Name comes to the grave all shiver and cold
and waits like coffee-spotted sugar.

Name goes to its grave a secret.

Name is anecdotal
evidence.

Name is the final name
in the coffin.

Name is not a person.
Name is barely a poetic cliché.

Name writes   someday I will love
anorexia nervosa   Please

Name   don't kill me   just bring me someplace
I can live.

& Name will cringe and flinch and and and I
will have my energy drinks

YOU ARE HOLY, YOUR [NAME*] IS HOLY, ETC.

Anorexia nervosa has no name.
Anorexia nervosa has no brain or shape.
Anorexia nervosa things in the shape of the name of the object it fills.

Anorexia nervosa ensures
she never looks the part.

Anorexia nervosa instead
takes up residence
in my ovaries.

Anorexia squeesez squeezes blood from my holes.
Anorexia attempts   am sharp
as a tack!

Anorexia nervosa reaches my brain.
Anorexia nervosa attends
to this poem.

~~The name of this~~

Anorexia nervosa is of my thighs.
Anorexia nervosa struggles
                    to name itselves.

AM SO SORRY

(an essay on   )

that a smart girl like me fell
for a ~~big~~ scam like that

and all she has to show for it
is eggs—really

two, scrambled, buttered—
plus, naturally

Yr affective
heft

&the blundering
crocodiles

that swim
In the mounds of yr cheeks.

I am so sorry

I have made you culpable.
Accessory   to

my anorexia.[1]

---

1. That big
bad word just

spits oil   from its   crevices

huh.
it weeps,

huh

whater you looking at?
everybody

knows, the paradigm
adds ten pounds.

//

eggs
as a concept

contain
several uncountable

truths.   e.g., egg:
Some people eat

a chicken's menstrual cycle
every morning.
e.g.,   egg: Some people

whip their whites and yolks
to cookies.   yum

e.g., Egg: Some people ~~adverb?~~ cry:
you call this

an egg, but
is an inadvertent chicken

stuck inside?

No one knows until you crack
it bleeds.

//

In terms of the bleeding chicken
I empathize—
bleeding sucks

and ~~I, too~~ till I start eating
I am also both dead and alive.

Maybe I am mixing my metaphors.
Animals attack

me with notions of killing,
outdoomed only by tales

of survivance.
Maybe this orderly reading

will figment an architecture
of apology.

Maybe I will stretch to fit
the girth of one ~~leg~~ long

diary. I am a smart girl
the sky is blue

albeit obfuscated ~~by~~
by motivational construction

paper. Outside, I imagine
a lumpening

of nests and a shittering
of trees and

you tear~~smile~~ your yoke [hold]
tight with compassion

~~and~~ social work my tits
into the shape of a sad

cannibal smile.
Like a mama turns a baby

bird to a container
for her juices.

IN A DREAM | M | ASKS IF I BELIEVE IN MERCY

Long ago a woman ten years my senior entered my body she entered two no three long fingers pale fingers beyond the door and with the key behind the door unlocked the button of the prior moment hands against breasts old man flesh hanged nippled knots this woman this author this surgical swagger this me which holds the story of her grasping fingers this crude cry out & face this fate worse than rape embarrassment sternum bold below shamesheet scabs sag formless i am wholly the wait of the name i have made for myself a heft deflates a heft deflates asks sarah are you sarah yes may I please have a glass of water

INTERRUPTED GIRL NARRATIVE

This girl who was black-haired
who was in my eyes
woman already made dash
Down the dimlit hall &
Attempted   herself before
A locked windowsill
And for all time after
We wondered "what
Pulled her
trigger?" The smuggled
Phone resting dead
Beside lost crayons and
Beads without strings
Or the boyfriend, presumably
Or otherwise parents
Or maybe, we this-
spared, it was simply
Something buried
Deep inside her chest
A bezoar a hair-tooth-
And-nail ball a crackling
Innard so long indisposed
And without exit
It animated first her feet &
Then legs &
Then hips &
Then stomach & you
See her projectile
body at the dimlit
hall-windowsill   oh
What it takes to become
A verb

DIFFERENTIAL DIAGNOSIS (12)

I made myself / a home /

in the center / of myself / I made

a dent /
a type /
a
hauntin
g / a
place /
a place
/ gorge
/ d / w
/ air

if I am us /

ing my power / 4 good / what /

to do

w / me

SELF-NARRATIVE (AS TRAGEDY PO E RN)

my body like a cold cruise animal. I lost my missile like a cruising fish. I lost my cold like a sought, blear bones. Nothing like the empty-making hunger that she animal compare. Time the hunger make an animal. Ah ah ah is the shape of the crouch. &AN shapea the bib. I encountering a small today. I am the shape and the shape and the fuzz was countering a fuzz I can scarcely believe. Would you believe if I maintained I mean, would you maim the tale. Would you mane the fuzz. Would you on my tailmake cruise my susceptible hole,,

DIFFERENTIAL DIAGNOSIS (13)

What exactly is required of me, I can't
do it.

I know nothing ever gets better
        too soon.
        without a fight.

A knock-down drag-out kind
a better.

Am I worth all I am capable of doing. This cruel
Knowledge.

RUNNING

If I were the person I thought I once was this spring evening I'd walk miles in my mother's old sweatshirt not out of hatred for my body but out of sheer sick cold. I would smell manure familiar to me and invented by the dairy midway between my home and the school where I learned I was fat. In that story, I become thin the way others grow up: gradually, adding with patience restraints, compunctions, ligatures, weights; steel where once was air. In my hometown is a correctional facility, another word for prison. When inmates escaped we kids hid in a dark corner of the classroom as in active shooter drills. Afterward we ate lunch. Today is any other March Wednesday. My arms with bumps or perhaps goosegrief   I am feeling perhaps even grief for the girl whose few words concerned the grief I mean the geese of her sister: good geese, kind. At the correctional facility she wound mandalas into ink at her bed while I, adjoining, jogged in place. You see there is a point that you get to when you forget to be hungry and begin to run into traffic. Sometimes I grieve that feeling the way my mother has tacit-promised to grieve me, if   At present the sun is melting and I am about to bike from this place to the apartment in which I keep my sad food and sometimes food for strangers. When I reach the traffic light I will consider my bicycle, legs, white shirt, bare arms now thick with ink. Being disordered is a manner of being out of order, that is, insequential, that is, inconsequential. I think of my mother. I love you. Your sweatshirt is in my closet.

DIFFERENTIAL DIAGNOSIS (14)

A pigeon is the story
of a bad dove. I dive

down center with the thinnest
gauge and leave a mark.

The drvoice bowels, "hey, you there!
No theory will protect you here.

Redemarcate the boundaries
of your knowing." Oh, I know

I am a wretch
to his glamour.

Could he make a person
of me yet. Yes, drvoice, I hear

you loud and clear. I know
the difference between odd

and awed.

COME, MY BELOVED

, and enter

The thunderdome.
I didn't intend for it to be this way, me
all disrespecting and farting and cussing
and bleeding on your creation. It's just:
my bad habits and me,
we have this thing, this pact:
as long as I stay alive, so do they.
You can see my struggle here, beloved,
because to end the bad's
to end the whole thing. And these days
I am simply unprepared to commit
suicide on the off
-chance it gets better

In conclusion, my beloved,
I am a cynic. I read
The Black Farm. I choose today
to stick to horrors within my
comprehension.
I know this may come as a surprise to you
but if I'm right about the pantheism,

what I've been holding in is really just you
hiding from yourself. I get it.
Some days I can hardly face the mirror, so I pretend
like I'm a car wreck
not a body.
Oh, beloved: what is your location.
There's a pileup on 395;

radio's sicker than a dying lung. I tend
to find my comprehension in between
my clavicle and spine. But who can say what's beyond
the bones.

ENDPOEM

Get fucked, my beloved.
Perhaps, no cats

have died in the con
struction of this product.

Perhaps we're still till
ing the lawn of the cradle.

The baby's mother comes
in alien green. Her name's

named Necessity:
Invention

is what doctors do
when necessity is dead.

Give me a black box.
Put in side.

SCRAPS

Upon what doom might my context dependent

And I was sucked in thick sick as a stomach.

I am trying to fill a basket.
But there's

You guessed it

A hole.

RQ: *Can you help me sink into a new mythology?*

A dent is a type of haunting.
Hauntings happen when
    one time is befallen
With another.

A dent

=

The sound the Monster makes
The tinny fracture

/

There is a permanent dent in my head.

I named the dent self-sabotage:
    All my shoes hit one
    place that never stops
    bleeding.

(It bled before the shoes.)

A crowd of shoes drop like hands to clocks.

Do you
find my
lines
insanely
sexy and
beautiful

A vent is the reverse of a dent.

A vent is a secret with a ticket to get in.

When I vent I invite you to eat me.
When I vent I form tea sandwiches with ham, provolone, and
mayonnaise. I am accompanied by small fruits.
Vents are bound to
time. Tighter to odor.

A rat once died deep inside a vent of mine.
But he rotted many times that winter
when the heat came on.

- I am helpless in the face
- Of my own legitimacy.
-
- I am hanged in the air
- The hair of my own bad
-
- Humor.

- *the map is not the terror story*[1]

1. Evelyn Berry, "the trans archive self-immolates," *Grief Slut* (Sundress Publications, 2023)

Anorexia is too holy to bear.

Anorexia is a gift I was given.

I received anorexia at a white elephant because it was the only thing left besides a

I would like to make a *gag gift* pun here

/

My vines belly and odious.

You don't know it's rotting until it's too late.

Poems are among the things praised for their sparsity and condemned

for their bloat.

Poetry can't account for the shape of this reckoning.

I send my regards from wherever this ends
up.

With your hands in my mouth
You recommend your body

-

And when my right mind finds me aching shivering with rigorous cold and numb to the arcane edges of my thoughts I have no doubt I will open my mouth thinking I can swallow it

Dents feature prominently in criminal-court proceedings.

I am so great at talking correctly.

/

I want to know what is the opposite of a stigma—

AFTER WARD

[on - sickness]

the waiting
room
is not a poem.
go home

ACKNOWLEDGMENTS

A humble & relentless thank-you to the journals that have shared poems from this collection, some in different forms:

Electric Lit: "Differential Diagnosis (1)," "Have you seen my autism?," and "When I taste blood"

Gasher: "Mise-en-scène"

Graphic Violence Lit: "Automythology (1)," "Automythology (2)," and "Half-Formed Girl Narrative"

Guest: "Differential Diagnosis (2)" and "Self-portrait as a sour jar of pickles buried deep beneath the earth"

Lammergeier: "Director's Cut"

MudRoom: "Diagnostician's Note"

Passages North: "in a dream | m | asks if i believe in mercy"

swifts & slows: "Differential Diagnosis (6)" and "Interrupted Girl Narrative"

The Temz Review: "Changeling Narrative," "Differential Diagnosis (3)," "impediment litany," and "a small something (2)"

Tilted House: "Substitution Poem"

X-RAY Lit: "Elephants think they are the size of dogs" and "Running"

&My utmost gratitude to the writer-friends who have [Mad]e this collection possible, including (but certainly not limited to): tommy blake, Ulysses Bougie, Rachel Fox, Twoey Gray, Sara Lefsyk, Valerie McLaren, Briar Ripley Page, Isaac Pickell, Elsie Platzer, Willa Smart, and wK.